ONE EVOLUTION AT A TIME

a special needs planning guide

Julia Nickerson

Copyright © 2016 Special Needs Forum, LLC, a Texas Limited Liability Company and Julia Nickerson
All rights reserved.
ISBN-13: 9780692782125 (Special Needs Forum)
ISBN-10: 0692782125
In accordance with the U.S. Copyright Act of 1976, the scanning, uploading, and electronic sharing of any part of this book without the permission of the author and publisher constitute unlawful piracy and theft of the author's intellectual property. If you would like to use material from the book (other than for review purposes), prior written permission must be obtained by contacting specialneedsforum.org. Thank you for your support of the author's rights.

Although the publisher and the author of this book have made every effort to ensure the information was correct at the time of going to press, the Publisher and Author do not assume and hereby disclaim any liability to any party for any loss or damage caused by errors, omissions, or misleading information, whether such errors or omissions result from negligence, accident or any other cause.

Neither the publisher nor authors provide through this book any legal, tax, or other professional advice. This book is intended to be a general overview only and is not to be relied upon for any specific legal advice. No legal advice or legal counsel is being provided to anyone via this book. Readers are cautioned not to take any action in reliance on the materials presented in this book without first consulting their own professional advisers. You should seek your own legal counsel to provide legal advice specific to your circumstances and state and local rules.

Dedicated to Evan and Stephanie

I have been deeply affected witnessing the struggles my brother and sister-in-law go through raising their son, R.E., who has autism. Their experiences inspired my passion for assisting families who have loved ones with special needs and for forming the Special Needs Forum. This book is dedicated to them: Evan and Stephanie Hart.

The cover photo is of Evan, Stephanie, their son R.E., and daughter Sena. While R.E. has autism, Sena has cerebral palsy.

Contents

Introduction ix

Chapter 1 Plan Like the Navy SEALs Train 1
Chapter 2 An Overview of the Government Benefits Programs You Need to Know About 11
Chapter 3 Supplemental Security Income (SSI) 19
Chapter 4 How to Maximize Your SSI Benefit 29
Chapter 5 Common SSI Disqualifiers 35
Chapter 6 Social Security Disability Income (SSDI) 47
Chapter 7 Medicaid 53
Chapter 8 Extra Benefits When a Parent Retires and/or Dies 61
Chapter 9 Transition at age 18: How to Stay in Control 69

Chapter 10 What You Need to Know about
             the Basics of Estate Planning ······83
Chapter 11 What are Special Needs Trusts
             and Why You May Need One ·····99
Chapter 12 Can a 529-ABLE Account Replace
             the Need for a Special Needs
             Trust? ······················113
Chapter 13 Putting the Estate Plan Together
             So It Actually Works············119
Chapter 14 Getting the Beneficiary of a
             Retirement Account Correct is
             Where Most People Make
             Mistakes ····················127
Chapter 15 Naming a Successor Guardian/
             Conservator··················139
Chapter 16 Leaving Instructions for Future
             Caregivers ···················145
Chapter 17 The Most Common Mistakes·····151
Chapter 18 Ten Evolutions . . . Take One at a
             Time ·······················159

            About the Author ············173
            Acknowledgments·············175

Introduction

Once I realized that people were starved for the information I had learned about special needs planning, I decided to write a book for the general population.

It took me two years to compile all the information in my head, get it down on paper, and then organize it in a fashion where people – not just attorneys, accountants, or financial professionals – could understand it.

This book is not written to be a treatise on every special needs planning issue. It is not written for professionals. You won't find citations to tax code sections, regulations, or case law. It also is not meant to provide legal advice to anyone.

Rather, it is meant to provide basic fundamental knowledge every family who has a loved one with special needs should know.

For more information about special needs planning, to find a local attorney, and for other resources, visit specialneedsforum.org.

CHAPTER 1

Plan Like the Navy SEALs Train

My Navy SEAL husband learned something in training that has stuck with him throughout his life and that has helped me, our children, and those close to us every day.

When my nephew R.E. was twelve years old, one of his favorite things to do was to run around and around *and around* the exterior of his house. While my three "neuro-typical" children and R.E.'s "neuro-typical" sister would play games together in the backyard, R.E. would run by himself, around and around and around the exterior of the house. He wouldn't mind if you ran around the house with him, but he probably wouldn't look at you or talk with you much. He would always have a big smile across his face though. R.E. has autism.

R.E. is the son of my brother and sister-in-law. He doesn't read much, but he can repeat extensive quotes from a movie he saw once, 12 months ago. If he decides he likes something, he will search YouTube videos and learn all he can about the topic — and repeat to you verbatim what he knows.

He loves to swim. When we were swimming in the pool last summer, I told R.E. that in order to do an underwater somersault he should tuck his knees up close to his chin. He didn't look at me when I told him this, and I didn't think he understood me or was even paying attention.

All of a sudden he tucked his knees up by his chin and put his face under water. In order to do the somersault, I had to push him in a circular motion. He would come out of the water laughing, take a breath, and go back under for another round. I would help him with his underwater somersaults over and over *and over* again. He is intriguing and a lot of fun, with a smile that will melt your heart.

R.E., like many children on the autism spectrum, is also a lot of work. There are many days with major breakdowns, some at home and others in public locations. Like many parents who have a child with special needs, my brother and his wife are dedicated parents who, through the gift of a child, have become selfless.

Some of the things that come with a child with special needs are confusion and a feeling of being overwhelmed. Once parents get the medical issues organized (if they ever do), then it's time to sort out the educational issues, and next comes socializing (not only for the child with special needs, but also for the siblings and parents).

The ordinary things in life that parents may take for granted, such as taking your child to a dentist for a teeth cleaning, are big concerns and obstacles for families who have a child with special needs. When R.E. needed to have some cavities filled, he had to be sedated in the hospital for the procedure. In most, if not all, communities across the United States, there is no one single resource that has all the answers or that can provide all of the referrals that families who have a child with special needs require.

This book is a resource for families who have loved ones with special needs like R. E. It addresses legal, financial, and long-term care concerns that I have learned from counseling hundreds of families who have loved ones with special needs. Many solutions that work for the "typical" family may not work for families who have a child with special needs. I have learned that most families with children with special needs know they need to become educated about legal, financial, and long-term care issues, but most don't really understand or even know what the issues are, let alone how to address and solve them. No one is to blame for this lack of understanding. The issues are somewhat complex, and the resources to help understand and implement them are limited. This leads to the feeling of being overwhelmed.

If you are one of these parents feeling overwhelmed, you have something in common with the United States Navy SEALs, and there is something you can learn from their training that can help you on a daily basis.

When I was in law school, my husband was in training to become a SEAL. This training program, called BUD/S (Basic Underwater Demolition/SEAL), is a six-month test of physical endurance and mental tenacity. I thought law school was difficult, but it was a walk in the park compared to what he was up against throughout BUD/S. He learned something there that stuck with him throughout his life and has helped me, our children, and those close to us every day. If you are feeling overwhelmed, I think this SEAL training technique can help you as well.

During BUD/S, a typical day's schedule was a wake-up call at 4:30 a.m., followed by a number of what they call "evolutions," such as a ten-mile timed beach run in deep sand, then a two-mile timed ocean swim followed at last by breakfast. They didn't just walk to the cafeteria for breakfast, they *ran* in crews of six or seven men, each crew carrying a 200- to 300-pound boat on their heads.

The reprieve of breakfast would be followed by more evolutions such as physical training ("PT") for an hour and a half on the "grinder," a skills test in the pool with their hands tied behind their backs, and on and on until 8:00 p.m. In the evening, the recruits often would study for an upcoming written test on topics such as dive physics or ensure their equipment would pass one of the upcoming surprise inspection tests. The next day and every day for months thereafter would be just as trying and filled with just as many "evolutions." There was even one week — called Hell Week — during which they didn't sleep for five and a half days. After that week, the top of my husband's head had been rubbed bald from carrying the boat.

As a bystander watching all of this going on, it was overwhelming to me, and I wasn't even a part of it. Instructors had the audacity to stand on the sidelines with coffee and donuts enticing the class members to give up, saying, "Come on over and grab a donut and some coffee." The problem was, if they did this — chose the donut over the physical torture and mental strain — they were out of the program and would never graduate as a SEAL. The instructors had a saying: "The only easy day was yesterday."

However, there was a coping skill that helped my husband get through each day and eventually graduate and earn his SEAL trident. His method, and that of many others who have gone through such rigorous training programs, was to only think about one evolution at a time.

Instead of looking at the day's schedule and being overwhelmed with the numerous tasks or evolutions, he only looked at the one evolution he was actually doing. Sometimes this meant just trying to get through the next mile of the swim or the next five seconds of a rigorous PT exercise.

My husband and I later learned that the example of the Navy SEAL training coping mechanism of taking "one evolution at a time" was actually a life lesson that could be applied over and over again. It taught us how to deal with *any* overwhelming situation.

While you may not be going through BUD/S training, many events in your day-to-day life become overwhelming if you lump them together. This is true with many of the issues associated with getting your family's and child with special needs' legal and financial life organized.

The first problem is you don't know what you need to do. You know there are government benefits available, but how do you get those? What are they? Where do you sign up? When is the best time to sign up? You've heard about special needs trusts, but you're not really sure what they are, if you need one, why you would need one, or how to go about getting one. This book is designed to help you answer these questions. The chapters of the book are arranged in a specific order to help develop a foundation of special needs planning and then to build on that foundation to secure the future for your family. At the end of this book is a list providing a specific order in which to tackle each important task.

When, not *if,* you have overwhelming moments, know that you are not alone. Remember to live and to plan like the Navy SEALS train, *one evolution at a time.*

CHAPTER 2

An Overview of the Government Benefits Programs You Need to Know About

Your child will be eligible for government benefits at age 18, but those benefits can be lost if not properly planned.

Government benefits are very important for people with special needs. Learning about these various government benefits and the applicable rules can be a daunting task. There is no one place to find information about all the benefits and answer all your questions. Rightfully, people can become overwhelmed when trying to learn about, apply for, and manage various types of government benefits. The key is to take it one evolution at a time.

WHEN WILL MY CHILD WITH SPECIAL NEEDS QUALIFY FOR BENEFITS?

Many people with a special need won't qualify for government benefits when the child is a minor because the parents' income and resources are counted. If the parents have a job and more than $2,000 worth of assets, a minor child who has a disability won't necessarily qualify for many government benefits.

Once a child who has a disability reaches age 18, that child will be eligible for government benefits based on his or her own record. However, these benefits can be easily lost. You as the child's parent must prepare in order to preserve these much-needed benefits.

WHAT GOVERNMENT BENEFITS ARE AVAILABLE TO MY CHILD WITH SPECIAL NEEDS?
There are four main government benefit programs:

> Medicare;
> Medicaid;
> Social Security Disability Insurance (SSDI); and
> Supplemental Security Income (SSI).

Medicare and Medicaid provide health insurance; SSDI and SSI provide monthly cash assistance.

WHICH GOVERNMENT BENEFITS ARE MEANS-BASED?
SSI and Medicaid are means-based programs. "Means-based" means that they have restrictions

and limitations on the amount of income and assets that the recipient with special needs can have in order to receive benefits.

If a parent passes away and as a result an inheritance passes directly to a child with special needs, SSI and Medicaid may be lost forever.

Even if you think that your family can provide for your child's lifetime needs, it is probably wise to position your child to qualify for Medicaid. Many programs that enhance the recipient's quality of life, including supported living and work environments, respite care, and in-home services, are only open to those receiving Medicaid.

WHICH GOVERNMENT AGENCIES ADMINISTER THESE BENEFITS?

All parents of a child with special needs have something in common. It doesn't matter if you have a child with autism, Down syndrome, cerebral palsy, intellectual disability, or one of the hundreds of other special needs. Every parent, at some point in time, wonders why it is so difficult to learn about, apply for, and manage all the different benefits.

Government benefits are available, but they are not managed by one single agency. SSI is administered by the federal government through the Social Security Administration. Medicaid is administered at the state level, and each state has its own agency. Medicaid Waiver rules are different in every state and, in some states, you have to contact the county in which you live to obtain Medicaid Waiver benefits. See Chapter Seven for more information on Medicaid and Medicaid Waivers.

Is there a conspiracy to make it difficult on purpose? No, but I do know that there is a lot of confusion because there are so many agencies that, for whatever reason, do not work together. Some families finally get all the details figured out in their state and then move to another state (or even another county within their same state) only to discover that the learning curve on many government benefits must start all over again.

One Evolution at a Time

It's wise to know which agencies administer which benefits. The chart below may help.

	Federal Agency	**State Agency**	**County Agency**
Medicaid, Medicare	Centers for Medicare & Medicaid Services	Each state has an administrative agency	
Medicaid Waiver		Each state has an administrative agency	Some states have a waiting list for each county
SSI, SSDI	Social Security Administration		Counties have their own SSA office

CHAPTER 3

Supplemental Security Income (SSI)

You can judge a society upon how it treats its most vulnerable citizens.

—Aristotle.

WHAT IS SSI?

Many believe the most important means-based government benefit program for an adult with special needs is Supplemental Security Income (SSI). It is a federal income supplement program administered by the Social Security Administration and is funded by general tax revenues (not by social security or self-employment taxes). SSI is important because in 39 states a recipient of SSI automatically qualifies to receive Medicaid benefits.

WHO QUALIFIES FOR SSI?

SSI is available to adults who have a disability. The Social Security Administration defines "disabled" as someone who is "unable to engage in any gainful activity because of physical or mental impairment that is expected to last for a continuous period of at least 12 months." If the disabled individual is earning more than $1,170 gross a month (2017 limit), then they don't meet this definition. A parent's income is not included in the determination if the application is for a person 18 or older.

Additionally, the person with special needs must not have assets, also referred to as "resources," worth more than $2,000. Certain assets are not counted in the asset worth calculation. A residence owned and lived in by a person with special needs does not count as an asset. A car doesn't count either. However, bank accounts, bonds, brokerage accounts, and received inheritances do count if owned by or titled in the name of the person with special needs.

SHOULD YOU APPLY FOR SSI?

Some families decide they are not going to apply for SSI because it is too much work or because they do not want to take charity from the government. All families should take a second look at why they should be applying for SSI. This benefit is not for you. It is for your child with special needs. It is not for the person who sits at home on the couch, watches television, plays video games, and eats potato chips while they could be working full time. It is for the disabled person with special needs.

SSI has been established by our society in order to take care of those who cannot take care of themselves. Our society *wants* to help those who can't take care of themselves. You should apply for SSI for the benefit of your loved one with special needs and not question it one bit.

WHEN SHOULD YOU APPLY FOR SSI?

If a child with special needs is about to turn 18, when should the parent or guardian apply for SSI for that child? You should apply during the month *after* the child attains age 18. Parents' income and resources won't be counted after the child becomes an adult. Payments start the month after an applicant becomes eligible.

If you apply *during* the month the child attains age 18, the parents' income and resources will be counted.

Example 1: Amy turns 18 on January 12, 2017. Amy's parents wait until February 1, 2017 to apply for SSI. The Social Security Administration won't require documentation evidencing Amy's parents' income and resources. Amy will be eligible for February payment and the payment will be made March 1, 2017.

Example 2: Amy turns 18 on January 12, 2017. Her parents file for SSI on that same day. Amy's parents' income will be counted, and thus she will not be eligible for the month of January. The Social Security Administration will require documentation evidencing Amy's parents' income and resources. While Amy will still be eligible for February payment and the payment will be made March 1, 2017, her parents will have unnecessarily gone through the ordeal of providing the Social Security Administration a lot of extraneous information about their own income and resources.

Thus, the best time to apply is the month *after* the child attains age 18. Keep in mind that if you wait until a couple of months or years after the child attains age 18 to apply, there is no retroactive payment.

Example 1: Amy turns 18 on January 12, 2017. Her parents file for SSI on February 1, 2017. It takes the Social Security Administration until September 2017 to decide to approve Amy's application. Amy will receive retroactive payment from February 2017 forward.

Example 2: Amy turns 18 on January 12, 2017. Her parents wait until June 2020 to apply for SSI. Amy is approved to receive SSI in October 2020. Amy will receive retroactive payment from June 2020 forward. Even though Amy could have been receiving SSI benefits since February 2017, she will never be able to receive payments for the time period between February 2017 and June 2020 since her parents waited years to file her application.

Many families think it is too much work to apply. You do not need to hire an attorney to help with your SSI application; however, if you are concerned about the application or think you may require legal advice, contact a local attorney who can help you. You will pay a small fee for an attorney to assist you with filing your application.

HOW DO YOU APPLY FOR SSI?
The best way to get started on the application process for SSI is to call the Social Security Administration at 1-800-722-1213.

An application for Social Security Disability Income (SSDI) can be found on the Social Security Administration's website (ssa.gov), but there is currently no online application for SSI. The Social Security Administration is working on a system that would allow people to apply for SSI online, but as of this writing, there is not one yet.

WHO MAY APPLY FOR SSI ON BEHALF OF A PERSON WITH SPECIAL NEEDS?

You don't need to be the court-appointed guardian or conservator of your child to apply for SSI or to be the representative payee. Generally the adult child should sign the application unless he or she is legally incompetent or physically unable to sign.

WHAT IS A REPRESENTATIVE PAYEE?

If a person is not able to manage his or her own benefits, that person will be deemed incapable and somebody can be appointed to be the *representative payee* for SSI purposes. This can be a parent, family member, or even a friend if there is no family. The Social Security Administration requires proof that the applicant is incapable. If there is a court-appointed guardian or conservator, that is enough proof. However, you can become a representative payee without a guardianship or conservatorship if the Social Security Administration determines a person is not capable of managing his or her own benefits.

Once appointed, the representative payee will receive payments on behalf of the applicant. Usually the SSI benefits are directly deposited into a bank account of the applicant. Examples of a correctly titled bank account that receives SSI for a disabled person: *Elizabeth Smith for Amy Smith* or *Amy Smith by Elizabeth Smith*.

WHAT IS THE MONTHLY SSI BENEFIT?

Once a person is approved to be a recipient of SSI, that person will receive a monthly benefit paid on the first of every month. The check can be payable to the recipient's representative payee and direct deposited into an account specifically set up to receive SSI benefits. The monthly benefit ranges from $1 to a maximum amount in 2017 of $735. As the federal government institutes cost of living adjustments, the maximum amount increases each year.

CHAPTER 4

How to Maximize Your SSI Benefit

As long as the person with special needs' actual cost of food and shelter does not exceed $735 per month, the person with special needs can avoid reduction of the monthly benefit with a "business arrangement."

The maximum SSI benefit may be reduced because of a number of factors. Many SSI recipients receive less than the monthly maximum payment. Many people receive two-thirds of the maximum.

Where and with whom the person with special needs lives can be factors that reduce the monthly SSI amount. When a recipient with special needs lives in the household of a family member who is providing both food and shelter, the SSI benefit is oftentimes reduced by one-third.

If the monthly pro rata cost of food and shelter for the person with special needs is above the monthly SSI maximum ($735 for 2017), then the Social Security Administration's position is that the individual with special needs doesn't have the ability to pay for the food and shelter. The SSA's policy is that the parents are paying for a portion and therefore are providing "In Kind Support and

Maintenance." This means that the Social Security Administration will reduce the $735 by one-third.

This can be avoided. As long as the person with special needs' actual cost of food and shelter does not exceed $735 per month, the person with special needs can avoid reduction of the monthly benefit with a "business arrangement." The person with special needs agrees to pay a pro rata share of the actual cost of food and shelter to the family with whom he or she is living. This rule only applies when the SSI beneficiary lives in his or her own household and someone in the household is related as parent or child.

When speaking with the SSA, inform them that the family has a business arrangement with the applicant and the SSI will be used to pay for the applicant's "fair share" of the food, rent or mortgage, and utilities of the home. Before your appointment with the Social Security Administration, you should know the monthly cost for all of your household members for the following expenses, as they will ask you about these during your interview: food, rent or mortgage payments, mandatory homeowner fees, property taxes, heating, gas and electricity, water, sewerage, and garbage.

Add up all the expenses and divide by the number of people who live in the home. If the amount of expenses per person is less than $735, then there is a good argument that there should be no reduction in the monthly benefit amount.

When you are preparing for these questions, you may think about overestimating the costs of these expenses. Always be truthful and remember it is not a good idea to overestimate.

If the expenses are too high, the Social Security Administration's policy is that the applicant can't pay for his or her fair share and therefore must be receiving support from a family member, which reduces the maximum by one-third. This is counterintuitive, but that is the rule.

If you have paid off your mortgage, you can report zero for mortgage expenses. This could help your child obtain the maximum amount. Again, counterintuitive.

Also, if a sibling is away at college, that child can still be included as a household member. The more members included in the household, the lower the applicant's fair share will be, so it is smart to include siblings for as long as possible.

CHAPTER 5

Common SSI Disqualifiers

Weighing the importance of employment versus SSI qualification is a dilemma for some families.

The most common disqualifiers or things that may make a change to the monthly SSI payment are:

1. Assets totaling more than $2,000 (2017 limit);
2. Inheritance;
3. UTMA (uniform transfer to minors account);
4. 529 accounts; and
5. A job earning more than $1,170 gross a month (2017 limit)

MORE THAN $2,000 IN ASSETS

Owning more than $2,000 can disqualify a person with special needs from receiving SSI. This limit is the 2017 amount set by the Social Security Administration. Once recipients start to receive

SSI, they (or their representative payee) are required to notify the Social Security Administration within ten days of a change of income, resources, or living conditions. If the Social Security Administration learns about a change of income or resources, it will determine if a change to the monthly SSI payment is warranted.

INHERITANCE

The most common and most concerning disqualification is the receipt of an inheritance from parents or grandparents who left money directly to a child or grandchild who is receiving SSI. Receiving an inheritance directly will disqualify that child from future Medicaid and other means-based government benefits. However, this doesn't mean you should disinherit the child with special needs. In fact, the child with special needs may have *more* need for the inheritance than children who don't have a special need. A neuro-typical child or loved one will (or should) be able to provide for themselves. An inheritance for them is an added bonus. An inheritance for a child with special needs may be a lifeline relied upon to maintain the child's lifelong standard of care. If you have a child, grandchild, or other beneficiary to whom you want to leave assets as part of an inheritance but are concerned about disqualifying them from benefits, consider creating a special needs trust, discussed in more detail in Chapter Eleven.

UTMA ACCOUNTS

Uniform Transfer to Minor Act (UTMA) accounts are commonly set up by parents or grandparents when a child is young, maybe even before a disability is known. Once a child with special needs turns a certain age, the UTMA asset is considered a resource of the person with special needs. This could be an SSI disqualifier. Each state has its own law as to when a UTMA account is considered a resource. In some states the age is 18, while in other states it isn't until age 21.

What do you do if you have a UTMA account for your child? There are a few options. However, each state has its own laws, so you should seek local counsel if you have one of these accounts and need to determine what to do with it.

Most likely, while your child is still a minor, you can use it for private primary and secondary school, college expenses, travel, extracurricular activities, health care, and dental expenses.

If the UTMA account has a small amount of money, it might be wise to withdraw and use the money for some of the person with special needs' expenses prior to applying for SSI.

If the account has a substantial amount of money, you should speak with your local attorney. There may be legal ways to change the account so that it is not a disqualifying resource.

529 PLANS

Section 529 of the Internal Revenue Code allows contributions into a state fund that can grow tax free. These 529 Plans, as they are called, are very common college savings vehicles, and many people set them up and fund them when a child is very young. What do you do if a 529 Plan has been set up and funded for your child with special needs?

Funds in a 529 Plan are typically considered a countable resource of the account owner. The account owner is the person who contributed to the

529 Plan (*e.g.*, the parent). Typically, a 529 Plan is not considered a countable resource of the beneficiary.

Distributions from a 529 Plan to a designated beneficiary who is receiving SSI used for educational expenses of the designated beneficiary are excluded as income in the month of receipt. If the designated beneficiary spends any portion of a 529 Plan distribution for a purpose other than educational expenses or no longer intends to use the funds for educational expenses, the funds are treated as income at the earlier of two points in time: (1) in the month the funds are spent or (2) in the month the individual no longer intends to use the funds for educational expenses.

Example: An adult with special needs, age 21, is the beneficiary of a 529 Plan. On August 5, the adult with special needs receives $1,500 from the 529 Plan. During the month of August, the individual spends $1,350 on educational expenses, $75 on groceries and intends to save $75 for "emergencies." The $1,350 for educational expenses is not considered countable income, the $75 on groceries and the $75 for emergencies are both countable income for August, and any portion of the $75 for emergencies that remains on September 1 is considered a countable resource.

WHAT IF I SET UP A 529 PLAN FOR MY CHILD WITH SPECIAL NEEDS, BUT MY CHILD IS NOT EXPECTED TO ATTEND COLLEGE?

If your child has a 529 Plan account but is not expected to attend college, you have a number of options to consider.

The first option is for you to withdraw the funds in the 529 Plan as the account owner. If you do that, you will owe tax on the earnings, plus a penalty equal to ten percent of the earning portion of the withdrawal.

However, there is an exception to the ten percent penalty if the designated beneficiary is disabled according to the IRS definition of disability, which can be a difficult standard to meet. Here again, we have different definitions of "disability," with the IRS's definition being different than the Social Security Administration's definition. According to the IRS, a person is considered to be "disabled" if he or she shows proof that he or she cannot do any substantial gainful activity because of his or her physical or mental condition. A physician must determine that his or her condition can be expected to result in death or to be of long-continued and indefinite duration.

A second option is to have the beneficiary take distributions. A beneficiary may take distributions from the 529 Plan. The beneficiary will owe tax on the earnings, plus a penalty equal to ten percent of the earnings portion of the withdrawal.

However, the exception to the ten percent penalty described above may apply if the beneficiary meets the IRS definition of disability. Note that these distributions are considered income for SSI purposes at the earlier of two points: (1) in the month the funds are spent, or (2) in the month the individual no longer intends to use the funds for educational expenses. If a countable distribution is retained into the month following the month of receipt, it is a countable resource.

A third option is to use the proceeds in the 529 Plan to pay for post-secondary vocational or technical training. If the designated beneficiary does not attend a traditional college, the money in a 529 Plan may be used to pay for post-secondary vocational or technical training at schools eligible for financial aid programs administered by the U.S. Department of Education.

A fourth option is to change the designated beneficiary of the 529 Plan. You can change the designated beneficiary of the account as long as the new recipient is a family member. That might be a sibling or step-sibling of the original beneficiary, or even a first cousin. Alternatively, the account owner can use the money to take college courses on a part-time basis, or consider saving the money for potential grandchildren.

If none of these options is a good choice for your family, you may be able to mitigate the tax consequences and the penalty of withdrawing the funds by donating proceeds of the account to charity and taking a tax deduction — if you itemize deductions.

WHAT HAPPENS TO SSI BENEFITS IF A PERSON HAS A PART TIME JOB?
SSI benefits can terminate if the recipient obtains a job at a substantial level of employment. In 2017, gross earnings averaging $1,170 or more per

month are typically considered substantial gainful earnings.

You also must be careful how you calculate gross income, as the Social Security Administration has a special rule. First you must deduct $20 as a general exclusion, then deduct another $65 for an "earned income exclusion," and then divide the gross income in half. Example: Amy, a long-time recipient of SSI, has received the maximum SSI benefit for years. In January 2017, Amy gets a job paying her wages. She receives $317 of gross wages in the month of January 2017. Amy must report this change to the Social Security Administration, and the amount she will receive in January 2017 for her SSI payment will be $619. In determining the amount of SSI Amy is entitled to receive, the calculation looks like this:

1. $317 - $20 = $297
2. $297 - $65 = $232
3. $232 divided by ½ = $116 (countable income)
4. $735 (SSI monthly maximum for 2017) - $116 (countable income) = $619

If a person receiving SSI begins to work and receive compensation, it is important to monitor the number of hours they work if they want to continue receiving SSI. If the monthly wages change at all, the representative payee is required to notify the Social Security Administration. Various ways exist on how to report a change in wages, including a wage reporting app you can download onto your mobile device. If the SSI recipient works too many hours, SSI could be reduced to zero, and that could in turn result in the loss of Medicaid, Medicaid Waiver, and other government benefits.

Most families want their loved one with special needs to become a contributing member of society and have gainful employment to the extent possible. Weighing the importance of employment versus SSI qualification is a dilemma for some families. If the average gross monthly income exceeds $1,170 (2017 limit), SSI may be lost; however, the individual with special needs may still be able to qualify for Medicaid under other criteria or be eligible for Medicare.

CHAPTER 6

Social Security Disability Income (SSDI)

While SSI is a means-based government program, SSDI is not.

Social Security Disability Income, commonly known as SSDI, is a different government benefits program from SSI. While SSDI and SSI are different in many ways, both are administered by the Social Security Administration. Only individuals who have a disability and meet medical criteria may qualify for benefits under either SSDI or SSI.

SSDI pays benefits based on past work history to people who are disabled. If someone has worked long enough and has paid social security taxes, that person may become insured and eligible for SSDI if he or she has a disability. For example, if you work for 20 years and then are involved in a terrible car accident that leaves you unable to work, you may be eligible to receive SSDI.

While SSI is a means-based government program, SSDI is not. In order to obtain SSDI, the recipient need not have resources limited to $2,000. Recipients may have significant assets and then later become incapacitated. Because they paid social security taxes for years before the incapacity, they may be eligible to receive benefits based upon the amount of earnings over their lifetime.

Many people confuse SSI and SSDI. In fact, many people who have been receiving benefits for years don't know if they are receiving SSI or SSDI. You should know what benefit you or your loved one receives. This chart helps clarify the difference:

SSI v. SSDI	
Supplemental Security Income (SSI)	**Social Security Disability Income (SSDI)**
Based on need	Based on work
Must have limited income and limited resources to qualify	Need not have limited resources to qualify
Maximum monthly payment in $700 range	Payment amount based on past earnings

Medicaid	Medicare after 24 months on SSDI
Paid on the first of the month	Not paid on the first of the month

Sometimes, the easiest way to determine if someone is receiving SSI or SSDI is to look at the day of the month on which the payment is made. If it is paid on the first of the month, it's SSI. If it is paid on any other day, it is SSDI.

CHAPTER 7

Medicaid

In 39 states, if your child with special needs qualifies for SSI, your child will qualify for Medicaid.

Medicaid provides health coverage to 60 million Americans. Medicaid is the portal to healthcare benefits and many other programs that provide a multitude of ancillary services that benefit someone with a special need.

Medicaid is funded by the federal government and each state. It is administered at the federal government level by the Centers for Medicare and Medicaid Services (CMS). At the state level, it is administered by specific state agencies and not by the Social Security Administration. It is very important for you to determine the state agency that administers the Medicaid programs in your state.

Remember, the Social Security Administration administers SSI. A state agency administers Medicaid. This causes a lot of confusion. Many people think that because they receive SSI and thus

Medicaid, the same agency administers both. Thus, many people mistakenly call the Social Security Administration to ask questions about Medicaid. Medicaid is means-based. Once a person with a disability is 18 years old, the government looks to the person with a disability's resources to see if they qualify, not to their parents' resources. A person with a disability can't own too much ($2,000 limit) or make too much ($1,170 per month gross) (2017 limits) – otherwise they won't qualify.

HOW DO YOU QUALIFY YOUR CHILD FOR MEDICAID?

In these states, if your loved one with special needs qualifies for SSI, they will automatically qualify for Medicaid:

Alabama	Iowa	New Jersey	Tennessee
Arizona	Kentucky	New Mexico	Texas
Arkansas	Louisiana	New York	Vermont
California	Maine	North Carolina	Washington

Colorado	Maryland	Pennsylvania	West Virgina
Delaware	Massachusetts	Rhode Island	Wisconsin
Florida	Michigan	South Carolina	Wyomoing
Georgia	Mississippi	New Jersey	Dist. Columbia
Indiana	Montana	South Dakota	

Once you apply for SSI in these states, you don't need to apply separately for Medicaid. Once an SSI application is approved for eligibility, the Social Security Administration will automatically notify the state's Medicaid agency. Medicaid eligibility will start the same month as SSI eligibility.

Seven states require the filing of a separate application for SSI and Medicaid. These are:

Alaska	Nebraska	Oregon
Idaho	Nevada	Utah
Kansas		

Some states use separate eligibility rules for Medicaid that are different from the Social Security Administration's rules for SSI. These states are:

Connecticut	Minnesota	Ohio
Hawaii	Missouri	Oklahoma
Illinois	New Hampshire	Virginia
Indiana	North Dakota	

MEDICAID WAIVER

What is a Medicaid Waiver? Does this mean that means-based testing will be waived? Can someone with too many resources still qualify for Medicaid if they receive a waiver? No.

A waiver is something a state applies for through the federal government. They are programs states can use to deliver and pay for healthcare services in the home or community, rather than in institutional settings such as hospitals. Each state has various

Medicaid Waiver programs that provide nursing care, attendant care, respite, therapies, adaptive aids, home modifications, service coordination, community living, employment support, and medical equipment.

Obtaining services under the various Medicaid Waiver programs also causes confusion. There is no federal website or phone number to learn about these programs. You will have to determine which programs exist in your state and then, in order to get access to such services, you may have to put your name on a waiting list or interest list. These lists vary in length depending on your state, the county where you live, and the particular waiver program. Many people will sit on these waiting lists for ten years. *You want to get on the waiting lists now, even if your loved one with special needs does not qualify for Medicaid yet.* People who work in your local school district's special education department should know about these waiting lists and be able to instruct you how to get your child's name on the specific lists in your area.

CHAPTER 8

Extra Benefits When a Parent Retires and/or Dies

The Disabled Adult Child benefit is a huge benefit and should be calculated when considering your lifetime financial plan.

When a parent of an SSI recipient retires and begins receiving his or her social security primary insurance amount, the individual with special needs becomes eligible to receive benefits as a "disabled adult child" or "DAC." This is very important, and it is a fact not widely known. As the parent of a child with special needs, you should familiarize yourself with the acronym DAC and learn what it means — it will play a big part in your long-term financial planning.

When a parent retires, a DAC is entitled to fifty percent of the parent's primary social security amount, subject to the family maximum. After a parent's death, a DAC is entitled to seventy-five percent of such parent's social security insurance amount, subject to the family maximum. The parent's social security benefit amount is not reduced because of this.

For 2017, the maximum social security benefit for a worker retiring at full retirement age is $2,687 per month. *Example:* Amy's father retires in 2017 with the maximum social security benefit. Amy qualifies as a Disabled Adult Child and is eligible to receive a portion of her father's social security benefit. Amy will be eligible to receive $1,343.50 per month (subject to the family maximum). Amy's SSI, with a maximum monthly benefit of $735, will stop and instead Amy will receive $1,343.50 monthly until her father's death. Once Amy's father passes away, Amy's monthly benefit will increase to seventy-five percent of the social security benefit, or $2,015.25 (subject to the family maximum).

WILL A DAC BE ELIGIBLE TO RECEIVE BENEFITS ON BOTH PARENTS' SOCIAL SECURITY RECORD?

It is important to note that a DAC is eligible to receive a portion of only one parent's social security insurance amount. When speaking with the Social Security Administration about this issue, you will want to select the parent who has the highest earnings record.

Another important factor is adoption and stepchildren. Sometimes, the person with the highest earnings record is a person who has provided for and taken care of the individual with special needs, but who is not the biological parent of the DAC. The Social Security Administration has special rules for determining if a stepparent, grandparent, or adoptive parent's earnings record can be used for DAC calculations.

WILL THE RECEIPT OF A RETIRED PARENT'S SOCIAL SECURITY BENEFIT CAUSE THE DAC BENEFICIARY TO LOSE SSI?
Yes, for many people, the amount a DAC beneficiary receives is great enough to disqualify such individual from receiving SSI.

IF THE DAC BENEFICIARY LOSES SSI, WILL THAT BENEFICIARY ALSO LOSE MEDICAID?
There is a special provision in the Social Security Act that provides that when a beneficiary loses SSI because of receipt of childhood disability benefits, for purposes of Medicaid eligibility, the DAC beneficiary is to be treated as if he or she were still

receiving SSI benefits, and thus remain eligible for Medicaid so long as he or she would be eligible for SSI benefits in the absence of the social security benefit. To continue Medicaid eligibility, the DAC beneficiary must continue to meet SSI asset limitations and income limitations (from sources other than DAC benefits).

ISSUES WITH NOTIFYING THE STATE MEDICAID AGENCY SO THAT MEDICAID IS NOT LOST

Remember that the Social Security Administration administers SSI and DAC benefits. The Social Security Administration does not administer Medicaid. When SSI recipients lose SSI eligibility because they begin receiving a greater monthly benefit as a DAC beneficiary, be prepared for the state Medicaid agency to discontinue Medicaid. A series of applications and proofs must be obtained from the Social Security Administration and sent to your state Medicaid agency to ensure Medicaid is not lost during this transition time.

Many people who work at the Social Security Administration and various local Medicaid agencies are not aware of this provision. Many families have been informed that their special needs loved one's Medicaid will cease due to DAC benefits. If you are told this, beware. Seek out the information you need to file the applications to ensure Medicaid is not lost.

TAKEAWAY

The benefits outlined in this chapter can become confusing — most likely because they are. The main takeaway is to plan for your child to receive the following means-based federal benefits for a lifetime:

1. Upon individual with special needs attaining age 18: SSI (2017 maximum: $735 per month);
2. When a parent of individual with special needs retires: fifty percent of the retired parent's social security insurance amount (use parent with the highest earnings record);
3. When a parent of individual with special needs passes away: seventy-five percent of the deceased parent's social security insurance amount.

This means you don't have to save for all the lifetime care of your child on your own. The DAC benefit is a huge benefit and should be calculated when considering your lifetime financial plan.

Another takeaway is to examine all of these potential benefits when considering your child's work conditions. Loss of SSI because of a job will also make the child ineligible to become a DAC beneficiary. While we want people with special needs to contribute the most they can and be contributing members of our society, we must weigh their job options with the potential loss of valuable lifetime means-based government benefits.

CHAPTER 9

Transition at age 18: How to Stay in Control

As a parent of a child with special needs, it is very important to know that when your child turns 18, you don't automatically have the same rights as you did when that child was a minor.

When a child with special needs turns age 18, he or she becomes a legal adult and the parents no longer have the legal right to manage medical care, control the educational plan, or to determine living arrangements.

Consider this scenario:

My child has severe disabilities. I have always been his caregiver and have cared for him at home. He just turned 18. I am being told I have no legal rights to make medical decisions for him or to consent to services on his behalf. I am not even able to know all that is going on with his medical treatment. His school tells me that he is in charge of making educational decisions now and I am not.

He is not able to understand what is needed, why it is needed, or what the consequences are if he doesn't receive services or medical treatment. He does not have the ability to communicate and serve as his own advocate. What do I need to do?

Parents who have a child with special needs often assume that they will automatically continue to be the legal guardian of that child when he or she becomes an adult at age 18 and continue thereafter for the child's entire life. As a parent of a child with special needs, it is very important to know that when your child turns 18, you don't automatically have the same rights as you did when that child was a minor.

Although it may be obvious to a parent that their child does not have capacity to make informed decisions, legally an adult is presumed competent unless otherwise deemed incompetent by a legal proceeding.

Legal options exist that are intended to protect adults with special needs from unscrupulous individuals and to allow someone else to make decisions on behalf of the person with special needs.

GUARDIANSHIP OR CONSERVATORSHIP

The most extensive and complete option is to obtain a legal guardianship of the *person* over the adult with special needs. This is not a guardianship of the *estate* (discussed in more detail in Chapter Ten). You want to avoid guardianship of the estate by creating a well-thought-out estate plan.

Obtaining guardianship of the person over an adult is not automatic. It requires filing a case with the court. The proposed guardian, usually the parents or a family member, files an application or a petition to take away the person with special needs' right to manage his or her own personal care. Those rights are transferred to the applicant by the court. Once appointed by a court, a legal guardian of the person is able to make medical, educational, and care decisions for the person with special needs and decide where that person should live.

Some states call these court cases *guardianships*. Other states call them *conservatorships*. While each state and county has its own specific rules for establishing a guardianship or conservatorship, the basic principles are the same.

The first step is for the proposed guardian to file an application with the appropriate court. The appropriate court will most likely be located in the county where the person with special needs resides.

YOU WILL NEED AN ATTORNEY

There are attorneys who specialize in guardianship cases. Hiring an attorney to assist with obtaining a guardianship is almost always required by the court, and the process can be expensive. Remember, however, that the information and help you receive from your attorney will help you avoid expensive mistakes in the future. If you think you are going to need a guardianship of the person, start planning financially for it in advance.

YOU WILL NEED A GOOD RELATIONSHIP WITH A DOCTOR

A doctor's certificate confirming the disability is a necessary part of the guardianship application or petition. The certificate will be the primary piece of evidence examined by the court to verify the disability and the person with special needs' inability to care for him or herself.

THE PERSON WITH SPECIAL NEEDS WILL HAVE AN ATTORNEY ALSO

The court will appoint an attorney on behalf of the person with special needs to protect his or her rights. This role is called an attorney ad litem or a guardian ad litem. This person will interview the person with special needs and make recommendations to the court. There are also costs associated with the attorney ad litem.

WHEN CAN YOU APPLY FOR GUARDIANSHIP?

If you are considering obtaining a guardianship of the person over your child, you can apply for it any time after your child turns age 18. Some families want to apply before age 18 to ensure not a day goes by without the parents being authorized to care for their child. Most states have statutory requirements as to how early someone can apply for a guardianship before a child turns age 18.

For example, in Texas, you won't be able to obtain the guardianship until the child actually attains age 18, but you can prepare and file your application six months before the child's 18th birthday. If you know you are going to need it, start working with an attorney three months prior to the 18th birthday to ensure all evidence is on file and ready by the 18th birthday.

Once appointed, a guardian of the person is responsible for monitoring the care of the person with special needs. The person with special needs must meet the definition of "incapacity" and is called the *ward*. The guardian need not use his or her own money for the ward's expenses, provide daily supervision of the ward, or even live with the ward. However, the guardian must attempt to ensure that the ward is receiving proper care and supervision. Also, the guardian is responsible for decisions regarding most medical care, educational, and vocational issues.

LESS RESTRICTIVE ALTERNATIVES

Whether to seek appointment of a guardian is obviously a complicated issue. A petition for guardianship should not be filed automatically just because a child has reached the age of 18. Parents or other potential guardians must carefully consider the person with special needs' individual circumstances, including strengths, weaknesses, needs, and best interests, before deciding to seek guardianship.

Remember, the Social Security Administration doesn't require a guardianship in order for someone to serve as the representative payee of an SSI recipient. If the person has special needs but is capable of making some but not all decisions, less restrictive alternatives such as a medical power of attorney or a supportive caregiver agreement should be considered.

MEDICAL POWER OF ATTORNEY

A Medical Power of Attorney, also known as a *Durable Power of Attorney for Health Care* or a *Health Care Proxy*, is a legal document that a competent person, the "principal," may use to name another individual, the "agent," to make health care decisions on behalf of the principal. The health care agent can be permitted to make all health care decisions for the principal once the principal becomes incompetent.

If your child has the ability to make his or her own decisions and can understand and comprehend what a medical power of attorney does, then by all means that is a better route than guardianship of the person. However, don't fool yourself about your child with special needs' level of comprehension or try to fool others.

A medical power of attorney should be considered for individuals who are *presently* capable of making decisions about their health care and wish to plan for anticipated *future* incapacity.

The proxy or medical power of attorney must be a written document that is signed by the principal, age 18 or older, and properly witnessed or notarized. The principal may revoke the document at any time.

Many families are confused about the difference between a guardianship of the person and a medical power of attorney.

Because a guardianship or conservatorship is an expensive court case and a medical power of attorney is a simple one or two page legal document, some use a medical power of attorney illegally. The typical illegal scenario is as follows:

> *The special education department at Amy's school has stated to Amy's parents that unless*

they have a guardianship over Amy, once Amy turns age 18, Amy will make all educational decisions for herself.

Amy's parents learn about a medical power of attorney. They find a form, fill in Amy's name, and then ask Amy to sign the form. Amy doesn't understand anything that the form says. Amy's parents then take the form to the school and inform the school that they, as the agents listed in the power of attorney, have the legal ability to make educational decisions on behalf of Amy.

Schools are faced with this situation all the time, and it is very sad. Parents are put in a difficult position because of the law, but the school is also put in a difficult position because the parents are abusing the law. First, the special education teachers and administrators know that Amy could not have understood what she was signing. Second, a medical power of attorney only allows parents to make *medical* decisions on behalf of their child. It does not allow them to make *educational* decisions. Third, this document only allows for the agent to act if the principal becomes incapacitated *in the future*. An individual who is incapacitated can't enter into a legally binding agreement. If the principal never had capacity to begin with, the document is legally void.

It is illegal to ask a person with a disability to sign a legally binding document that they don't understand. It's also unfair. We should never ask an incapacitated individual to sign a legal document we know the person doesn't understand simply because it's easier than doing it the right way and obtaining a guardianship.

SUPPORTIVE DECISION-MAKING AGREEMENT
Another less restrictive alternative to guardianship or conservatorship is a "Supportive Decision-Making Agreement." A Supportive Decision-Making Agreement allows the individual to stay in control but grants someone the ability to help make care decisions.

This chart helps explain what a supporter under a Supportive Decision Making Agreement can do:

Can	Can't
Help someone understand their options, responsibilities, and consequences of their decisions.	Make the decision
Help obtain and understand information relevant to decisions that need to be made	Make the decision
Communicate decisions to the appropriate people.	Make the decision

Legislation passing the authorization of Supportive Decision-Making Agreements is relatively new and as of this writing, only the state of Texas has a law authorizing this option. You may want to ask your local attorney if this type of agreement is legal in your state.

The person signing this agreement should understand what is being signed, just like discussed above regarding the medical power of attorney. Often, this type of agreement is done in conjunction with a medical power of attorney.

CHAPTER 10

What You Need to Know about the Basics of Estate Planning

Americans who have loved ones with special needs have some extra hurdles to jump in order to protect, improve, and enhance the lives of their beneficiaries.

WHAT IS ESTATE PLANNING?

Lew Dymond is one of the country's greatest and most well-known estate planning professionals. He has a way of taking complex materials and making them understandable to everyone. The best definition of estate planning I know, I learned from Lew:

> *I will do whatever it takes to ensure that when I am gone family harmony is realized and the inheritance I leave protects, improves, and enhances the lives of my beneficiaries.*

Lew credits this definition to his colleagues at WealthCounsel, a group that consists of estate planning attorneys from across the country. I love this definition because it uses positive terms like "protect," "improve," "harmony," "enhance," and "whatever it takes." Nowhere in that definition does it talk about "tax planning" or "passing down" large dollar values. Of course, if there is a tax issue, then tax planning should be *one* goal of estate planning.

ESTATE PLANNING IS FOR EVERYONE.
Estate planning is not just for one economic class. All Americans (not just wealthy Americans) need estate planning. Americans who have loved ones with special needs have some extra hurdles to jump in order to protect, improve, and enhance the lives of their beneficiaries. Estate planning is complex and shouldn't be done without trusted and experienced legal counsel.

THE NEED
Many people have heard about special needs trusts and have decided that is what they need in order to protect their child with special needs. Some parents think that such a trust is the only estate planning they need to protect a person with special needs, but in reality they need more. They need an estate plan. Such a plan consists of documents such as a will, a revocable living trust, a special needs trust,

beneficiary designations, and many more legal instruments that ensure their assets are titled correctly and pass pursuant to the intended goals. The right estate plan can be a gift to your family.

EVERYONE HAS AN ESTATE PLAN — IS IT THE CORRECT PLAN?

If you haven't created an estate plan of your own, the government has one for you. The government's estate plan involves probate and can be expensive and time consuming, relies on a judge and the judicial system to make decisions, and causes unnecessary drama. Often, the government's estate plan favors the government over the child with special needs' inheritance. Children with special needs may never be able to compensate for your failure to implement a well-thought-out estate plan.

> *Real Life Example: Sarah's father died when she was just 3 years old. Her father paid for a life insurance policy and named Sarah as the beneficiary. The life insurance company wouldn't pay out the policy because the named beneficiary was a minor. Sarah's mother spent years in court*

and tens of thousands of dollars in court costs and attorney fees in a guardianship of the estate case.

Guardianship of the *estate* is needed if a minor or an incapacitated adult receives an inheritance (including life insurance or retirement benefits) outside of a trust. Guardianship of the estate is very expensive and an administrative hassle. One of your goals after reading this book should be to never let a guardianship of the estate happen to your family. In some states, guardianship of the estate may be called by a different legal term. Whatever the legal term is in your state, remember this: you don't want it.

Estate planning isn't the most fun thing on your "to do" list. Know going in that creating your plan is something you have to spend some time doing and spend some money on to get done correctly. Also know that it is less expensive and not nearly as time consuming as a guardianship of the estate.

Without an estate plan in place, your loved ones won't inherit your assets in the way that you want. For families who have children with special needs, this is especially important because you will also disqualify them for valuable government assistance.

Because none of us knows when we might die or become incapacitated, it is important to plan early for your child with special needs, just as you would for a minor child. However, unlike most beneficiaries, your child with special needs may never be able to compensate for your failure to plan. Make sure your estate plan provides for all the people you love. Doing so will ensure that you leave a positive legacy for your entire family.

GOAL: Make it a goal that the transition of your financial wealth will be as easy as possible for your family.

WHAT IS THE PURPOSE OF A WILL?
Most people know, or think they know, what a will does. A will is a legal instrument signed with all the correct legal formalities that states a person's wishes as to how assets will be transferred upon death. Most of the time, after a will is signed, it lies dormant in a safe, safety deposit box, or on a shelf someplace in your home.

People try to forget about their wills after they sign them. Oftentimes, someone signs a will and years go by without any changes being made, even though the people listed in the will have changed dramatically, assets have changed dramatically, laws have changed, and lives have changed. When someone actually dies, the will becomes very important, so it is crucial to keep it updated as circumstances change.

Heirs may go to the bank or ask the family financial advisor about an account, only to learn that the account is frozen. They will be told that in order to "unfreeze" the account, they need something called "Letters Testamentary." After asking what Letters Testamentary are, they will be told to hire a probate attorney.

WHAT IS PROBATE?

Probate is a court process to transfer a decedent's assets after someone dies. A lawyer prepares legal paperwork to open the probate court case. As part of this probate court case, the decedent's original will must be located and filed in the county and state in which the decedent lived. There will be at least one court hearing during which people named in the will may attend and provide evidence to a judge. Court documents, often called Letters Testamentary, are issued to the person determined by the court to be responsible for handling the decedent's affairs, giving that person authority to deal with financial matters, etc. This is usually the person named in the will as executor, or someone who steps forward to assume responsibility if there is no will. Without this authorization, it can be very difficult if not impossible to deal with a deceased person's accounts.

Probate can be simple or complex depending on (1) in which state the decedent resided, (2) the makeup of the assets, and (3) how good the will is.

A CAUTION ABOUT "DO-IT-YOURSELF" WILLS
Probate attorneys love online do-it-yourself forms and people who don't sign their wills in an estate planning law firm. If your will is not prepared with necessities and signed with formalities, probate is *not* an easy process.

Internet wills are being advertised a lot lately. In a way, this is good because it encourages people to start planning. However, an internet will won't be an effective estate plan for most people. Many people are surprised to learn that their will controls a relatively small percentage of their overall estate. Life insurance policies, retirement plan accounts, and sometimes bank and brokerage accounts (depending on how they are titled), aren't distributed pursuant to a will. Without proper estate planning advice, most people incorrectly designate the beneficiaries on these policies and accounts, necessitating a court-supervised guardianship of the estate to control the proceeds if a minor child or a child with special needs is designated as a beneficiary. Remember what was said above: one of your goals should be to avoid a guardianship of the estate.

Online legal sites contain disclaimers stating that they "are not acting as your attorney," "do not practice law," "do not give legal advice," and that their "information is not guaranteed to be correct, complete, or up-to-date." The courts that license attorneys across the country will not allow any licensed attorney to give such disclaimers. Like online legal sites, this book is a resource, and while helpful, it doesn't provide you with specific legal advice direct to your circumstances — you need to hire a lawyer to assist you.

Without proper estate planning counsel, many issues go unasked about and unplanned for. When using an online service, you must fill in answers to legal questions without receiving any help from an attorney who knows the law and is experienced in handling issues like yours. In the end, you may be setting something up that you did not intend or that is not appropriate for your specific situation.

The reason why many probate attorneys love online and do-it-yourself forms is because it makes for a more difficult probate process, which in turn equals more legal fees for the attorney. I've been in the probate court where my clients, whose parents or other family members failed to plan, are asking the judge, "Why does it have to be this difficult, especially when so much of an inheritance for the benefit of a child with a disability is lost to legal fees, bond fees, and court costs?" The only reply a judge can give is, "If it had been set up correctly, it wouldn't have been this difficult and expensive."

You have a choice. You can set it up correctly for your family with proper legal advice. You can try to set it up correctly with do-it-yourself forms. You can do nothing and allow the expensive and time-consuming default rules to govern what happens to your family's inheritance. Planning is too important to ignore, and it is too important and too complicated to go about without professional advice and assistance.

PROBATE TAKES SOME TIME

Assets are frozen while waiting to go through the probate process. In some states, the probate process can take years. In other states, probate only takes months. Nonetheless, while the process is going on, assets may be frozen and unavailable to use for a beneficiary with special needs.

PROBATE IS PUBLIC

Probate is public, meaning all legal documents are filed and become a public record. In many counties, these documents can be found online. When working through the probate process, most of the time a list of the decedent's assets becomes a court record.

People can find out who the beneficiaries are in a probated estate and what and how much they received. This can become problematic for beneficiaries with special needs who may become vulnerable to predators. Many people want to avoid probate because of its public nature.

WILLS V. REVOCABLE LIVING TRUSTS

For years, revocable living trusts (trusts that can be changed or amended during the lifetime of the person who sets them up) have replaced wills as the foundation for all estate planning. While there are some estate planning attorneys who continue to cling to wills, many attorneys who focus on estate planning agree that living trusts are better foundational documents than wills.

A revocable living trust is a legal agreement where the G*rantor* (the person making the trust document) contributes assets into a trust. The trust will be controlled by a *Trustee* for the benefit of a *Beneficiary* or *Beneficiaries*. Many times, when a person creates a living trust, they serve in all three positions — as the *Grantor*, the *Trustee* and the *Beneficiary* during their lifetime.

After the Grantor signs the living trust document, the Grantor then contributes to the trust by retitling assets so that they are owned by the living trust.   The Trustee manages and distributes the living trust assets for the beneficiary according to the written instructions outlined in the trust document.

If the Grantor becomes incapacitated and can no longer manage his or her finances, a person named in the document as a successor trustee steps in and manages the assets for the beneficiary. Since the Trustee holds legal title to the assets in the trust, no court needs to interfere in the financial affairs of the incapacitated grantor.

Upon the death of the Grantor, the living trust becomes irrevocable and the successor trustee named in the trust document steps in and begins to manage the living trust assets and distribute them to the named beneficiaries. No court or probate proceeding is needed to transfer ownership of assets owned by the living trust.

There are many pros to a living trust based estate plan. There are some downsides as well. For some people, wills are more appropriate because of eldercare planning or the makeup of assets. You should understand the difference and work with your estate planning attorney to decide which works best for your family situation.

RECAP

Remember Lew's definition of estate planning:

I will do whatever it takes to ensure that when I am gone family harmony is realized and the inheritance I leave protects, improves, and enhances the lives of my beneficiaries.

In order to accomplish these goals, you will most likely be working with an attorney experienced in special needs planning to set up documents such as a will and/or a living trust and a special needs trust.

CHAPTER 11

What are Special Needs Trusts and Why You May Need One

Oftentimes, the one heir who needs an inheritance more than any other is a child with a disability.

A special needs trust is designed to manage assets for the benefit of a person with special needs without causing that person to become ineligible for means-based government benefits. If your loved one with special needs requires or is likely to require governmental assistance to meet basic needs, do not leave an inheritance directly to that individual because it will cause that person with special needs to become ineligible for SSI and Medicaid.

Instead, establish a special needs trust. Federal law permits you to create a special needs trust that can hold assets for the benefit of a person with special needs without disqualifying the person with special needs from SSI and Medicaid.

Planning is important because many adults with disabilities will rely on government benefits for support. Remember, if the person with special needs owns more than the limit (currently $2,000), they will lose eligibility for many government benefits. Medicaid and other public benefits programs will not pay for everything your child might need. Some families make a big mistake and disinherit a child with special needs so that the child can qualify for SSI and Medicaid. Oftentimes, the one heir who needs an inheritance more than any other is a child with a disability. An inheritance for the benefit of a person with special needs can be made payable to a special needs trust. The trust can be governed by a person you name and the sole beneficiary is the person with the disability. It can pay for items not provided by government assistance and other resources.

PAYBACK PROVISIONS

Not all special needs trusts are the same. Some require any unused assets in the trust to be paid back to the government upon the death of the beneficiary. This is commonly referred to as a "payback provision." These payback provisions are not necessary for a trust that holds inheritance.

It is not uncommon to find payback provisions in a special needs trust when there should be none.

Make certain your family doesn't make this mistake. No payback provisions are required in a trust that holds an inheritance. Attorneys who don't specialize in this field might make this mistake. This is another reason to find an attorney who specializes in estate planning specifically for families who have a loved one with special needs.

PRIVATE SPECIAL NEEDS TRUSTS

Special needs trusts can be public or private. A private trust is prepared by your attorney. You choose the terms of the trust and determine who the trustee will be. The trustee is the person or persons who will manage the trust for the benefit of the beneficiary. Your chosen trustee determines the trust investments, can elect to hire an investment manager, and is also the person who makes distributions.

THE TRUSTEE

Your trustee can be a trusted family member who is good with managing money and has a love for the beneficiary with special needs. If you don't have a trusted family member who is good with money or if you think a professional would be a better choice for the job, you can name a trust company to serve as the trustee of your privately created special needs trust. A trust company is in business to manage assets of a trust. Many banks and brokerage firms have trust departments that serve as trustees of hundreds, if not thousands, of trusts. Trust officers know how to invest money and how the specific rules of trust distributions work.

Before naming a trust company, you should interview the trust officers to determine if it's a good fit. Any good trust company will want to know a little about the goals you have for the beneficiary.

THE CARE MANAGER

Another good idea is to name a Care Manager, a person who can work with the corporate trustee to communicate the specific needs of the beneficiary. This is especially important if you are naming a trust company to serve as trustee.

One trust company we know serves as the trustee of a trust whose beneficiary loves tennis balls. The beneficiary lives in a group facility, but he has a shed to hold all his tennis balls. The corporate trustee works with the Care Manager to ensure the beneficiary has the resources to buy a new can of tennis balls every week. Once, there was a problem with the shed. The lock was broken and the beneficiary couldn't get in to play with his tennis balls. The Care Manager let the corporate trustee know about this incident, and the corporate trustee made sure a locksmith was called and a new lock purchased.

The reason I recite the story of the tennis balls is because a trustee, whether a professional, a family member, or a trusted friend, is not just there to pay the ongoing monthly bills. Life continues even after the death of parents, and life brings occurrences for which we can never plan. You want a trustee you not only trust, but also one who will work with your Care Manager to ensure your child's needs are truly being met.

FAMILY MEMBER AS TRUSTEE

Many people name a family member as trustee of their special needs trust. They may name an adult sibling or adult cousin of the beneficiary as trustee. This family member trustee most likely grew up with the beneficiary, knows the highs and lows of the beneficiary's life, and is intimately involved with the concerns and issues the beneficiary faces. A close, caring relationship between the trustee and the beneficiary can be a huge benefit.

The relationship can also cause huge problems. The specific investment and distributions rules of a special needs trust are complex. Understanding and complying with them can be challenging. It takes time, patience, and effort for a nonprofessional to learn all the details of how to administer a special needs trust properly. A close caring family member or friend may not want to spend time learning about how a special needs trust functions and may not want to spend time maintaining the trust accurately. Resentment may build up over time, which is probably not the intention of the grantor when naming the loved one to serve as trustee.

SUCCESSOR TRUSTEES

A special needs trust can have its own succession plan. If the named trustee is unwilling or unable to serve, you can name one or more alternate trustees so that a court doesn't have to be asked to appoint a successor.

Alternatively, the trust document can grant the current trustee the ability to name a successor trustee. If the family member trustee decides that serving as trustee is overwhelming, there can be an option for that person to resign and name a successor without the necessity of court involvement. To make the trust even more flexible, there could be provisions so that the family member can stay on as Care Manager, which would allow the family member to work with the successor trustee to ensure the beneficiary's needs are being met.

THE TRUST PROTECTOR

When establishing a special needs trust, many people ask, *"What steps can I take to ensure the trust will work even after I am gone?"*

One option is to include a *trust protector*. A trust protector is a person named in the trust document who can do certain things even after the trust-maker is deceased. For example, if a trust officer who has served a family's special needs trust for years decides to move to a different trust company, the trust protector can ensure that the trust officer stays with the trust.

The role of trust protector is different from that of a trustee. Representing the long-term intentions of you as the trust-maker, the trust protector can provide guidance and oversight as the trustee carries out your wishes. A trust protector can also watch over your trust to ensure that it is not adversely affected by any changes in the law or circumstances.

For example, the Social Security Administration may change the way it interprets certain words in your special needs trust or certain administrative provisions of how means-based government benefits are allocated. If the special needs trust does not have such updated language, it could be harmful for the beneficiary. A trust protector can overcome this problem by updating the trust so that it complies with the most recent regulations.

TRUSTEE COMPENSATION

Compensation for a family member trustee is another matter to consider when creating your own private special needs trust. Should the family member trustee be paid compensation for serving as trustee? Compensation is for the trustee's time spent on administering the trust. If you have an individual serving as trustee, you may want to limit or define the amount of compensation he or she is entitled to receive. Even if your special needs trust document allows for a family member trustee to take compensation, many family member trustees decide not to do so.

Corporate trustees have compensation schedules. Many charge an annual fee based on the value of the assets in the trust, often between one and one and a half percent. Often there is a minimum dollar value a corporate trustee will require as principal in the trust or a minimum annual dollar fee.

Whether or not you want your family member trustee to be paid compensation for time spent on administering the trust is a question you should discuss with your attorney when creating your special needs trust.

Compensation is different from reimbursement. Of course your trustee can be reimbursed for accounting, legal, or other out-of-pocket expenses required to administer the trust.

POOLED TRUSTS

Special needs trusts don't have to be private. You can join what is called a "pooled" trust. These trusts "pool" the resources of many beneficiaries. Every state has its own pooled trust that is administered by a nonprofit association.

There are pros and cons to choosing a pooled trust, but these trusts may not be the right choice for many families. One benefit is that they are administered professionally. This can also be a con. Pooled trusts are only as good as the nonprofit administering them. If there is management turnover or financial problems, your loved one's trust is stuck with all these problems until they can be worked out. You can't change the trustee of a pooled trust like you can with a private trust.

Some pooled trusts only distribute assets at certain times of the month. This can be a problem for a beneficiary who may require more frequent distributions.

Pooled trusts can also become very expensive. Many have hidden fees and expenses, so find out exactly what the fees consist of before joining. In addition, many pooled trusts will not agree to own real estate and other nontraditional investments. If your inheritance includes nontraditional investments, a private individual special needs trust may serve you better than a pooled trust.

CHAPTER 12

CAN A 529-ABLE ACCOUNT REPLACE THE NEED FOR A SPECIAL NEEDS TRUST?

While the 529-ABLE legislation was a good start, these accounts come with many limitations.

The Achieving a Better Life Act of 2014 established a new savings vehicle for disabled people that is commonly called a 529-ABLE account. A disabled but mentally competent person can have more than $2,000 in a 529-ABLE account without losing eligibility for SSI or Medicaid. Like traditional 529 accounts, principal in a 529-ABLE account grows income-tax free, making them, upon first sight, attractive.

While the 529-ABLE legislation was a good start, these accounts come with many limitations, and for most families, they don't replace the need for a private third-party special needs trust. They are receiving a lot of press, so it is important to know the downfalls before deciding if these accounts are right for your family.

First, the beneficiary is in charge of the account. While a child is a minor, a parent can manage the accounts; however, once the individual with special needs attains age 18, they will be in control. If you have a beneficiary who can't manage finances, this is a problem and rules out these accounts altogether. Some will think that they can manage these accounts for their individual with special needs because they have a guardianship or conservatorship. Remember, guardianship of the *person* is what many have or want. Guardianship of the person gives the guardian control over medical care, living arrangements and other personal care needs. Guardianship of the estate gives the guardian control over finances and comes with an extreme amount of court involvement. Guardianship of the estate is expensive and an administrative hassle. Most people want to avoid guardianship of the estate.

Second, these accounts are good for small amounts, but if they hold over $100,000, the beneficiary is back to being disqualified from means-based government benefits. You might think you can bypass this rule by creating multiple accounts, but the law only allows one account per beneficiary.

Also, there are limitations on what the assets can be used for once distributed out of the 529-ABLE account. The beneficiary can't use the funds to go to a movie, purchase clothes, or go on a vacation—things that many families would want their child to save up for. Rather the funds must only be used for disability related expenses. Because this legislation is so new, the law is not set yet on how this will be interpreted. Hopefully further regulations can be put into place to define 'disability related expenses' but as of this writing, it is unclear and thus may cause much confusion as people start to open, fund and begin making distributions from these accounts.

Finally, the nail in the coffin against these accounts is that they work like a payback trust, making them not good for holding an inheritance.

So what can you use a 529-ABLE for? This is a good question. They are good for special needs individuals receiving SSI and Medicaid who can manage a small amount of money. For example, part-time workers who want to save some of their income can contribute into a 529-ABLE account. Also, if Medicaid recipient receives a small inheritance or settlement outside of a special needs trust, it can be placed in a 529-ABLE account to ensure benefits are not lost. But remember, the person with special needs, not a trustee, manages this account.

Because these accounts are getting so much publicity, it is likely that many will open the accounts not knowing all the downsides, only later to seek assistance on how to get out of them.

CHAPTER 13

Putting the Estate Plan Together So It Actually Works

At your death, some of your assets may not be governed by the wishes you have expressed in your will and/or living trust.

You have learned about a number of legal instruments that make up an estate plan, including a will, a living trust, and a special needs trust.

A will or living trust states where you want assets to go upon your death. For those assets you want to pass for the benefit of your loved one with special needs, a will can state that the beneficiary is your special needs trust. Your estate plan would look like this:

For those families who choose a living trust, your estate plan would look like this:

If you are doing this yourself and you stop there, most likely you will end up requiring your loved one with special needs to have a guardianship of the estate. Remember that thing you are trying to avoid? To ensure your estate plan is set up correctly, you should learn about how your life insurance and retirement accounts pass.

BENEFICIARY DESIGNATIONS
At your death, some of your assets may not be governed by the wishes you have expressed in your will and/or living trust. Retirement accounts and life

insurance are examples of assets that pass at death in accordance with a separate beneficiary designation. These assets have contractual arrangements with a financial institution. When individuals set up a retirement account or purchase life insurance, they are asked to fill out a beneficiary designation form. What is listed on this beneficiary designation form controls who receives the assets upon death.

Many people forget to review and make proper changes to their beneficiary designation forms. They get a new job that has a 401(k) plan and are asked to fill out a lot of paperwork. That beneficiary designation form lies in the stack of documents that must be filled out and gets overlooked. These beneficiary designation forms are very, very important.

Many families who have a child with special needs have worked hard to build up a significant IRA or 401(k). Prior to obtaining professional legal advice, most have named their child with special needs as either a primary or contingent beneficiary of their retirement account. Not having professional advice when naming the beneficiary of a hard-earned retirement account can have a disastrous effect on a person with special needs' life.

What happens if one of the beneficiaries you name on your retirement account or life insurance policy is a person with special needs? Will they lose their ability to receive government benefits? How will the distributions from the tax-deferred retirement account be taxed? These are complicated questions, but they shouldn't be overlooked if you have a child with special needs and a significant or even a moderate amount of assets in your retirement account.

Many people purchase life insurance to help take care of a minor or a child with special needs in the event of a parent's death. When you buy a life insurance policy, you are asked to fill out a beneficiary designation form. You can list a primary person, such as a spouse, and a contingent person if the primary person fails to survive you or if you die together.

If you list a minor child or a child with a special need, that child will have to deal with a guardianship of the estate. Remember, one of your goals is to ensure that your family will never have a guardianship of the estate.

If you take the extra step of getting the beneficiary designations aligned with your estate plan, the plan would look something like this:

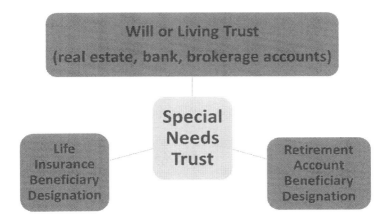

One of the most important things you can do when planning for your child with special needs' future is to take the time to sit down with a professional to map out how your beneficiaries should be listed on all of your investment and insurance forms. The time you spend now can make a huge difference down the road.

CHAPTER 14

Getting the Beneficiary of a Retirement Account Correct is Where Most People Make Mistakes

Taking the time to determine what to write down on your retirement account beneficiary designation form may lead to a significant income tax savings over the life of a special needs loved one.

You can name a special needs or supplemental needs trust as the beneficiary (or the contingent beneficiary if your spouse is still alive) of your retirement account. However, the proper kind of trust must be named. If you create the wrong type of trust or put the wrong language on the beneficiary designation form, these could be costly mistakes that limit the amount of income tax deferral your loved one with special needs is able to receive over his or her lifetime.

This is a complicated area of the law even for most attorneys. In fact, many attorneys get this wrong — and it is a huge mistake. If you have a significant amount of savings in your retirement account, it is worth learning about and finding an estate planning attorney who is experienced with how distributions from retirement accounts are taxed upon death.

Traditional IRAs and 401(k)s are tax deferred, meaning the participants haven't paid any income tax on the contributions. The government's policy reason for allowing this tax deferral is to encourage us to save for our own retirement (so we won't have to rely only on the government to provide for us after retirement). This policy, however, doesn't extend to perpetual tax deferral. At some point in time, the government forces us to take distributions from these tax-deferred accounts and pay income tax.

When someone dies with funds remaining in that person's tax-deferred IRA, 401(k), or other qualified retirement account, there are rules requiring the beneficiary to take distributions and pay the income tax. Often, the beneficiary will have the option of taking all the funds out immediately (or over a five-year period) and paying all the income tax. Alternatively, certain beneficiaries are able to extend the tax deferral, not have to pay the income tax immediately, and allow the principal to continue growing with the tax deferral.

INCOME TAX BENEFITS OF NAMING AN INDIVIDUAL AS THE BENEFICIARY OF YOUR RETIREMENT ACCOUNT

Owners of retirement benefits are commonly advised to designate spouses, children, relatives, and other individuals – *not* trusts – as beneficiaries of retirement benefits. This is because a *person*, with a definable age and life expectancy, is able to *stretch* out the distributions they are required to make from an inherited IRA over their life expectancy. By only taking out a minimum amount that the IRS regulations require, the owner allows the principal amount remaining in the inherited IRA to continue to grow without needing to pay income tax on the principal.

For example, an individual beneficiary who is 18 years old when the retirement account owner dies has a life expectancy of 65 years according to the IRS's single life expectancy table. Instead of taking a lump-sum distribution of the entire value of the retirement account and paying income tax on it in the year of the retirement account owner's death, the 18-year-old beneficiary has the option to receive a distribution of only 1/65th of the value of the account every year and pay income tax only on that 1/65th each year. That continued income tax deferment can be significant over time. In the above example, a $500,000 IRA with a five percent annual growth rate calculates to $1.4 million in distributions over the life of that 18-year-old beneficiary.

Being able to *stretch out* the benefits of an inherited retirement account is commonly referred to as a "stretch" in the industry. If you have a significant amount in your IRA, you may want your child to be able to "stretch" and can arrange your estate plan with this specific goal in mind.

However, what if you have a child with special needs? That child can't receive retirement benefits and still qualify for SSI and Medicaid. You've been told that a special needs trust should hold the assets for a child with special needs. The problem is, a trust is not a person with a definable age and life expectancy, and therefore trusts are often not able to obtain the "stretch" treatment.

CAN A SPECIAL NEEDS TRUST BE A BENEFICIARY AND ALSO GET THE STRETCHED INCOME TAX DEFERRAL?

Is there a way to get the stretch income tax treatment and not be disqualified from SSI and Medicaid?

A properly drafted "see-through" trust with special needs provisions can serve as the beneficiary of a retirement account, and the stretch income tax treatment is then available. The see-through trust is an exception to the traditional rule that a trust has no life expectancy. If we are able to *see through* the trust and identify the beneficiaries, then a life expectancy can be determined and the trust can get the stretched income tax treatment.

There are two types of see-through trusts: the "conduit" trust and the "accumulation" trust. In the conduit trust, only the life expectancy of the current beneficiary is considered. The trustee must immediately distribute the required minimum distributions to the current beneficiary. These distributions must be counted as either income or a resource and may disqualify the recipient from means-based government benefits.

SEE-THROUGH ACCUMULATION TRUSTS — BEST FOR A CHILD WITH SPECIAL NEEDS

In an accumulation trust, when the required minimum distributions are received from the retirement account by the trustee, they are not required to be paid out immediately to or for the benefit of the trust beneficiary.

If you want your trust to serve as an accumulation trust, you must look at the life expectancy of the oldest possible beneficiary, whether that beneficiary is a current beneficiary or not. When designating who would receive the remaining assets in the trust if the disabled person were to die, you would not want to include any charities (charities have no life expectancy) or individuals significantly older than the intended initial beneficiary.

Because this type of planning may be different than what a family would want for their nonretirement assets, retirement stretch trusts designed to be accumulation trusts can be drafted as stand-alone documents, and their purpose is to do one thing: serve as the beneficiary of a retirement account.

PENSIONS

While traditional pensions are not as common as they once were, families with pensions should be cognizant of what election to make, especially if they have a child with special needs. With an IRA or 401(k), the participant has his or her own account and can see that account value rise and fall over time. A pension differs in that there is no defined contribution amount and the participant has no account balance. Rather, participants are promised a certain amount of monthly payment, usually based upon their years of employment and years of highest compensation.

Most small employers do not offer a pension. Also, many large publicly traded employers have terminated their pension plans. The pension plans still in existence are typically those obtained through government employment (*e.g.*, city, state, federal, military, teachers) and through larger employers with plans that have been in existence for a significant period of time.

Each employer plan will have its own rules, but traditionally, at a certain time period before your retirement age, you will be given the opportunity to elect which option you want for your payment. One of the options is to take the full amount of your pension over your life. Oftentimes, there is a second option to take a reduced amount over the lives of you and your spouse. Many people select this option because they want to ensure their spouse receives the pension even if the participant dies.

What does this have to do with special needs? Sometimes, there is a third option: to take a reduced amount over the life expectancy of the participant's and the participant's child with disabilities' life. This could end up being a significant financial benefit to your child with special needs. If you are a participant in a pension, don't forget to find out if your plan has this option and analyze whether it makes sense for your family financially.

RECAP

It is difficult enough to deal with estate planning issues associated with a loved one with special needs who qualifies for SSI and Medicaid. It becomes especially challenging when a loved one with special needs is intended to be the beneficiary of a significant retirement account. Taking the time to determine what to write down on your retirement account beneficiary designation form may lead to a significant income tax savings over the life of a loved one with special needs.

Not being aware of the problems when these various laws intersect can result in unnecessary income tax, a loss of the child with special needs' government benefits, or both. Selecting a professional with knowledge about these types of rules is essential when looking for an attorney to represent your family. If you trust your lawyers but they don't understand this area of law, ask them to co-counsel with an attorney who does. Because the laws surrounding the stretch are federal laws, an expert outside of your state can help make sure your local attorneys get this done correctly.

CHAPTER 15

Naming a Successor Guardian/Conservator

No one person has to do it all, not even you. Consider creating a Care Team now while you are alive and well.

One of the most important things parents of a child with special needs can do is to legally document which person they want to take care of their child if they are no longer able. If your child is going to need a guardianship or conservatorship at age 18 or if you are already serving as your adult child's guardian or conservator, you can name a successor guardian or conservator in the event you are no longer able to serve.

For parents who have a child with special needs, the task of naming a guardian or conservator to take care of children can be extra difficult. Often, there is no one who has developed the patience or is willing to deal with the life sacrifices it takes to manage the ongoing caregiving that a child with special needs requires.

The successor guardian you name can be the person who will make the best health care, educational, housing, and care decisions for your child with special needs. Maybe they live in your same community and have the maturity, patience, and time to take care of your loved one. They do not have to also be financial decision makers and understand all the administrative requirements of your special needs trust. If the person you want to name as guardian is not good with financial management, doesn't want to learn, or is overly confused with the administration of means-based government benefits, then you can name someone else to take care of the assets left to the special needs trust.

Many people think the only person who could serve as guardian of their adult child with special needs is an adult sibling. However, adult siblings have lives of their own and may harbor resentment if they are forced into taking on such responsibility. Speak with your family about this role and develop a plan together so that an adult sibling or other family member views serving as a welcome opportunity and not a burden.

No one person has to do it all, not even you. Consider creating a Care Team now while you are alive and well. This team can consist of people who truly love and will advocate for your child, even if you are not there. Your Care Team can meet annually, semi-annually, or quarterly. Talk about what your goals are for your child with special needs and who will be responsible for what if you can no longer manage everything. A team makes everything feel more manageable if the members are working together on a common goal.

CHAPTER 16

Leaving Instructions for Future Caregivers

While you may know all of the specifics of your child's life, your successor probably does not have it all memorized.

Think of the knowledge you have gained spending a lifetime caring for your loved one with special needs. You have certain goals for them. You have some ideas on where you want them to live (or don't want them to live) when you can no longer care for them. You know about their medical care, which doctors they see, and which medications they take. Hopefully you know a lot about the benefits and supports they receive. If all that knowledge is only stored in your head, there will be no record if something happens to you. Why not document this knowledge and these goals?

You can create a guidebook about your loved one with special needs. Some people call this a Memorandum of Intent or a Letter of Intent. Whatever you decide to call it, the purpose is to communicate and document your preferences and guidelines regarding the care of your child with special needs. It is like a set of instructions to guide future caregivers and trustees.

This set of instructions is not intended to be legally binding, but it may be one of the most important and most relied upon sets of documents you prepare (and maintain) in your planning process.

If you have already established a Care Team, they can help contribute to these instructions. Try to avoid strict demands because, as circumstances change, such demands may be difficult to carry out.

Don't worry if you don't get everything down on your first draft. You can always add to these instructions in the future. Also, use your own words, and those words don't have to be fancy.

I like binders with tabs. When I have things set out in order with a table of contents in a binder with tabs, it helps to make me feel organized. Some people hate binders and instead keep important documents stored online. There is no specific format you need to follow to create your set of instructions. Figure out a way to establish your instructions so that it helps you feel organized and then get started.

The first part of your instructions may include the biographical information of your loved one with special needs: full legal name, date of birth, place of birth, and social security number. This may seem trivial, but if you start with the basics, at least you are getting started. It should also include the child's parents' full legal names, dates of birth, places of birth, and social security numbers. Many benefits a child with special needs can receive will be based upon their parent's records, so including the parents' information is important. While you may know all of these things, your successor probably does not have it all memorized.

Which people in this world will your successor guardian or trustee need to contact? Think of them all and include their contact information. Include relatives, friends your guardian or trustee can rely on, professionals such as your attorney and accountant, case manager, care providers, and physicians.

Some other "chapters," "files," or "tabs" in your binder may include financial information, living arrangements, programs, benefits, abilities, and personal preferences. Also, as part of your guidelines, you can write a personal statement to those people who will have responsibility after you are gone. This statement may include instructions, but also expressions of encouragement and thankfulness.

Realize that once you complete your initial draft, the contents will continually need updating. Your loved one's life will change and as such, your instructions should change. One suggestion is to review your instructions annually (e.g., on or around your loved one's birthday) and make any necessary updates. Don't get overwhelmed with making your instruction guidebook. It doesn't have to be perfect. Work on it slowly over time and keep adding to it to make it better. Take it one evolution at a time.

CHAPTER 17

The Most Common Mistakes

A person who never made a mistake never tried anything new. – Albert Einstein.

As you go through this process of learning and preparing to get yourself and your goals organized, it can be a productive exercise to learn what does not work. We all make mistakes and we can learn from the most common mistakes that people make when planning for a loved one with special needs.

Mistake 1: Disinheriting the Individual with Special Needs

Many people with special needs rely on SSI, Medicaid and other means-based government benefits. Some people disinherit their child with special needs, the child who needs their help most, to protect that child's means-based public benefits. But these benefits only provide basic needs. It is unnecessary to disinherit a child with special needs.

Mistake 2: Procrastination

Because none of us knows when we may die or become incapacitated, it is important that you plan for a beneficiary with special needs early. No one wants to think about death. Planning for it is not a fun activity—thus, many procrastinate.

Mistake 3: Do it Yourself

Some people think they can do this alone without the help of experts. Making a mistake in this context can be very expensive and can cause your child with special needs to be stuck with the effects of your 'do it yourself' plan for life.

Learning only from friends instead of professionals or from professionals who do not make this type of planning a focus can also be devastating. For example, many families will open a 529 ABLE account because they have heard about them from their friends or a 'professional' who has no sincere focus on special needs planning. For many families with a child with special needs, a 529 ABLE account won't be a good choice.

Mistake 4: Pay-Back Provisions
Another frequent mistake occurs when a special needs trust includes a "pay-back" provision rather than allowing the remainder of the trust to go to others upon the death of the child with special needs.

Mistake 5: Failure to Properly "Fund" the Plan
If sufficient assets are not available for the child with special needs' lifetime support, don't rely on others to pick up the financial burden for you. Instead, invest in life insurance. Oftentimes permanent life insurance is the perfect vehicle for this purpose, particularly if the parents are young and healthy such that insurance rates are low.

Mistake 6: Failure to Update and Maintain
Many people put a plan in place and then never look at it for years. The truth is, your plan needs to work at an uncertain time in the future when no one knows what your assets will consist of, what your priorities will be, what your family situation will look like and what the law will be. Revisit your

plan frequently and keep it maintained so that it will work when it needs to.

Mistake 7: Failure to Coordinate Beneficiary Designation Forms

Remember, retirement plan assets, life insurance and annuities pass pursuant to a beneficiary designation form. The beneficiaries listed on these forms can coordinate with your overall plan. The last thing you want to do is purchase a large life insurance policy only to disqualify your child from means based government benefits.

Mistake 8: Failing to Protect the Child with Special Needs from Predators

An inheritance from parents who fund their child's special needs trust by will rather than by revocable living trust is in the public record. Predators are particularly attracted to vulnerable beneficiaries, such as the young and those with limited self-protective capacities. When you plan with trusts rather than a will, you decide who has access to the information about your children's inheritance. This protects your child with special needs and other family members, who may be serving as trustees, from predators.

Please don't make these costly mistakes with your own child with special needs. Make a commitment to get things in order and then ease into it---take each step *one evolution at a time*.

CHAPTER 18

Ten Evolutions ... Take One at a Time

The important things are knowing what the evolutions are, becoming committed to getting them accomplished, and taking them one at a time.

Remember from the beginning of this book that one of the things that comes with a child with special needs is confusion and a feeling of being overwhelmed? After reading and educating yourself on all the things you need to do to help protect your loved one, you could decide to be overwhelmed. However, a better approach is to tackle each issue as a Navy SEAL does – one evolution at a time.

You have already accomplished one big step. Just by reading this book, you have become extremely knowledgeable about what issues are out there that can harm your child. You have learned that it won't serve your child to ignore these issues. You have also learned that the issues are complicated and that you will need professional help.

The ten evolutions outlined in this chapter will help you build that security around your child that you so desperately crave. For some people, they will tackle the ten evolutions within six months. For others, it may take a couple of years to accomplish them all. The important things are knowing what the evolutions are, becoming committed to getting them accomplished, and taking them one at a time.

While working through these evolutions, you may find more that need to be added to this list of ten. Great. I don't profess to know it all. Add your new evolutions to your list and tackle them one at a time.

ONE: FIND WHAT MEDICAID WAIVER
PROGRAMS EXIST IN YOUR STATE

Determine what Medicaid Waiver programs exist in your state and get on the local waiting list. It can take ten years or longer for your loved one's name to reach the top. If you haven't already done so, get your loved one's name on these lists now.

If you already have your name on the Medicaid Waiver programs lists in your area, great! You have already accomplished the first evolution. If you haven't done this yet, go back to Chapter Seven on Medicaid to remind you of what you need to do. Then, take an afternoon to research your state- and county-specific Medicaid Waiver programs. With this research in hand, write a letter or call the various places.

If you still think you need help to accomplish this task, ask a friend who has a child with special needs to help you. You can also ask your child's school. Many of the teachers in special education departments know where to call to get on the waiting lists.

TWO: SAVE
Start saving *now* to pay for future professional service experts. You may want a good lawyer with lots of experience and knowledge in this specific area of the law. Find the right experienced special needs attorney for your family and have savings earmarked just for paying professional fees for expert assistance. When your child reaches age 18 and you have money saved, you can afford to hire an attorney to assist with guardianship (or conservatorship), if necessary. You will need an estate plan, perhaps guardianship, and maybe some professional assistance with getting approved for certain government benefits. Your savings plan will enable you to afford professional assistance when going through

the necessary steps to ensure all benefits for your child with special needs are obtained.

THREE: FIND AN EXPERIENCED ATTORNEY AND GET YOUR ESTATE PLAN IN ORDER

Find a local attorney who is skilled in estate planning and specifically estate planning for special needs. Don't just rely on an attorney who does contracts, real estate, litigation, *and* probate. Just like doctors who specialize, attorneys specialize as well. The law is so vast, attorneys can't know everything. If you can't find someone in your area who specializes, tell your attorney you want them to co-counsel with an expert who can assist having it done properly. It is important to find someone you trust and enjoy working with, as they should serve as your attorney for a long time.

If you are concerned about the cost of an experienced attorney, do some legwork to relieve your concerns. Once you have located the attorneys you want to represent you, contact their office and ask for an *initial consultation*. During this consultation, you will not obtain free legal advice, but you will be able to provide a general overview of your specific situation to the attorney. The attorney should provide you with an estimate of the price to update your estate plan. If you aren't ready to outlay that price yet, you will know how much you need to save. You can then calculate how much time it will take you to save before you can hire the attorney.

Many people who are not familiar with working with attorneys are fearful of contacting a law office and are fearful of the potential price of hiring an attorney. Decide to get over this fear. Attorneys are people just like you. Estate planning attorneys who help families with a loved one with special needs want to help you.

You should know a few things though about how law firms work. First, when you make your first call, don't expect to speak with the attorney. You want to make an appointment to talk with the attorney (often times this is called an initial consultation). There may be a price for this initial consultation or it may be complimentary.

When you go to your initial consultation, don't expect the attorney to provide you with legal advice. Attorneys won't provide legal advice until you have hired them. The purpose of the initial consultation is to get to know the attorney to see if you trust them and like them. The attorney or someone on the attorney's team like a paralegal will get to know a little about your family and your concerns. They should also tell you a price range of how much it will cost to hire them. If you are ready to hire the attorney, then tell them. If you are not ready to hire the attorney yet because you still need to save to afford their price, tell them and then make it a point to actually save for their services. I have had plenty of clients who tell me they can't afford to hire our law firm now, but they will save up and contact me in a few months or a year.

Once you find the attorneys you trust and have saved enough to afford their professional services, hire them to get your estate plan in order. Since you've read this book you know that everyone needs an estate plan, not just wealthy people. You also know that an estate plan is not just a will. Your attorney can help you decide if you want a living trust-based plan, update your life insurance and retirement account beneficiary designations, and make sure the title to all your other accounts is styled correctly. Of course, your attorney may also create a special needs trust that will serve as the beneficiary of any assets you want to pass to your child with special needs. Your attorney may also create a separate document naming who you want to serve as your child's guardian if you can't serve. Everyone's situation and goals are unique, and your attorney will be able to guide and counsel you to develop an estate plan that fits your family.

FOUR: PROVIDE ENOUGH FINANCIAL RESOURCES
Work with a financial advisor to determine exactly how much savings or insurance would be sufficient to support your family if something happened to you. If you don't have a financial advisor, ask your estate planning attorney for a recommendation. Estate planning attorneys work with financial advisors on a daily basis and will know someone who is the right fit for you, your family, and your financial circumstances. Your financial advisor can help with your savings plan and keep your financial goals on track.

If you are uncomfortable hiring a financial advisor, realize that you will be the one managing your family's investments. Take this seriously.

If you don't have sufficient savings and investment resources, then make sure you have enough life insurance. Life insurance is one of the best ways to get money into a special needs trust. Term insurance is inexpensive, but it expires after a certain period of time without building up any continued value. Permanent or whole life insurance is more expensive, but if you have a child with special needs, you may want to consider it to guarantee that needed resources will be available for your child upon your death.

Once your life insurance is in place, have your life insurance agent work with your estate planning attorney to ensure the beneficiary designation form is compliant with your overall plan.

FIVE: CONSIDER GUARDIANSHIP OF THE
PERSON AND ALTERNATIVES AT AGE 18

When children with special needs reach age 18, they become legal adults. Parents are no longer entitled to make decisions about an adult child with special needs' education and personal care unless they petition a judge to become the child's legal guardian or conservator.

Guardianship or conservatorship of the person is not the same as guardianship of the estate. You want to avoid guardianship of the *estate*, but you may want to obtain guardianship or conservatorship of the *person*.

Before deciding on guardianship or conservatorship of the person, decide if your adult child with special needs has the ability to understand and is legally competent to sign a power of attorney or a supportive caregiver agreement. Less restrictive means may be available that allow a supporter to help an adult with special needs make decisions.

SIX: APPLY FOR SUPPLEMENTAL SECURITY INCOME AT AGE 18 AND MAINTAIN BENEFITS

Your child will be eligible for government benefits at age 18, but you must prepare to preserve much-needed benefits. If your child with special needs owns more than $2,000 of nonexempt assets, he or she will not qualify for Supplemental Security Income ("SSI"), and in turn, not necessarily qualify for Medicaid.

When your child turns age 18, plan to apply to receive SSI. If your child is over age 18 already and you have not applied for SSI, plan to file the application now.

Once a parent retires, means-based government benefits change. If your special needs loved one goes to work earning a salary, government benefits may also change and you will need to report these changes to the Social Security Administration.

SEVEN: BUILD YOUR CARE TEAM

Start building your Care Team now and having meetings. You will be amazed at how the team will grow and change over time. Also, you will feel reassured that others are there who will take over if you can't.

EIGHT: WRITE YOUR INSTRUCTIONS
FOR FUTURE CAREGIVERS

Start compiling your instructions to guide future caregivers and trustees. When your Care Team meets, share the location and general contents of these instructions.

NINE: INVESTIGATE LIVING ARRANGEMENTS

With neuro-typical children, they leave home and make their way in this world at age 18 or in their early 20s after college. With children with special needs, many stay living at home into their 30s, 40s, and 50s. If your child has a normal life expectancy and is expected to live longer than his or her parents, there should be a succession plan for living arrangements. Maybe this is in the home of a sibling or trusted family member or friend. Maybe it is in group home or one of the amazing living facilities that exist specifically for individuals with special needs. Costs vary, and some you may not be able to afford. Don't wait until you are ready for a nursing home to investigate living options for your adult loved one with special needs. It will bring you peace of mind knowing sound living arrangements exist for your loved ones even if they are not with you.

TEN: REVIEW AND UPDATE

Do not think that once you accomplish steps one through nine you can just check the items completely off your "to do" list. In reality, estate plans need to be maintained over time as your life changes, your family changes, your priorities change, and the law changes. Your financial plan needs to be updated. Guardianships or Conservatorships require an annual report. Receipt of government benefits requires annual reports and maintenance. Your guidebook on your loved one with special needs should also be continuously updated. Find an attorney who not only creates your plan, but actively reaches out to you to ensure it is maintained. If you haven't had your plan updated recently, get it updated and keep it that way. Continually meet with your financial advisor and your Care Team.

If you are stuck on an area, go back and re-read that chapter. This is a journey that you are taking over your life. Keep getting your evolutions accomplished, even if it is just one at a time.

About the Author

Julia Nickerson is an attorney who has helped hundreds of families plan ahead legally and financially for a loved one with special needs. She has been practicing law and helping families with estate planning since 1997 and is Board Certified in Estate Planning and Probate Law by the Texas Board of Legal Specialization.

Julia's passion for special needs planning stems from witnessing the struggles her brother and sister-in-law go through raising their son with autism.

Julia helped found the Special Needs Forum, which advocates for and educates families on issues relating to their loved ones with special needs.

Learn more about the Special Needs Forum at specialneedsforum.org.

Julia, her husband Jim, and their three children live in Austin, Texas.

Acknowledgments

We talked about the Navy SEALs who, because they have to work together, are often called "the teams." Like the SEALs, it takes a team to raise a child with special needs, and it has taken a team to get this book in order.

I have spent hours with my team of attorneys and colleagues gathering the knowledge to impart in this book, especially those at WealthCounsel, ElderCounsel, Marbridge Foundation and Nickerson Law Group. Those who sponsor and contribute to the Special Needs Forum live events have opened my eyes to many important issues in special needs planning. Thank you for your support, your knowledge, and your friendship.

Without truly getting to know the love and the heartache that exist for the families I have represented, I would have never been able to learn about the issues for which so many crave knowledge. You have all blessed me, and this book is as much yours as it is mine.

Evan and Stephanie, thank you for granting me the permission to include your story. Mom and Dad, thank you for reading early manuscripts and offering invaluable advice. To my three children Will, Mimi, and Wes, thank you for granting me the time spent in the office instead of with you. Lastly, a most grateful thank you to my husband Jim's unwavering support.

Made in the USA
Columbia, SC
24 September 2017